The Good Road

By

Ibran Shaikh

Introduction

A family on vacation lose their son. A truck driver's last ride. A girl chasing hope. This is a life affirming journey, across a local highway, and into the heart of an unseen India, where acts of great compassion are shown to strangers.

Pappu is a truck driver. Supporting his parents and extended family is beyond his means. Now, he has been presented a plan. An accident will be staged. Pappu will "die". Insurance payments are substantial.David and Kiran, a middle class urban couple, with their son Aditya, are on a holiday. Aditya will be accidentally separated from them during a brief halt at a Dhaba. And his loss will only be discovered several hours, and several hundred kilometers later. They must double back to find him. Poonam is an 11-year old-year-old child from the city. She is looking for her grandmother, living in a town at the end of this highway. Tired and hungry, Poonam wisely stops at the Topaz, what seems to be a small garment dying unit.Aditya will be found by a local dhaba owner, and put onto Pappu's truck. Has Aditya found a new and unlikely home on this truck? Later, when it is too late, Poonam will discover that the Topaz is not quite the place for her. She will be confronted, forcefully, with the very same choices she is running away from. Which way will this young girl turn? And Pappu, looking for answers to balance his need with those of this little boy, will find a new strength and conviction within.

State Highway 378 on the border of the Rann desert, Gujarat. The highway is as beautiful as it is unsettling. Accidentally separated from his parents, the city-bred 7 year-old Aditya finds himself in the care of Pappu, a truck driver and his assistant Shaukat, both operating just beyond the law. As a friendship develops between Pappu and Aditya, the police close in on him, dwindling his options. The truck driver is torn between his sense of responsibility to care for this lost boy and his own future. Poonam is a 9 year-old girl looking to hitch a ride to her grandmother's home. Tired and hungry, she unwittingly ends up in a brothel in the middle of nowhere. As the realization of where she has found herself dawns on her - she is forced to choose between staying with the new friends she makes or finding a ride on the highway. The characters on The Good Road meet each twist, turn, dip and rise, in the road and in their fates, with stubborn hope. This is a journey across tarred roads and into the heart of an unseen India, where acts of great compassion are shown to utter strangers.

Chapter 1

The story begin with ‘Hello’ said by Pappu

‘How are Mom and Dad?’

They are fine. said by Pappu’s wife

‘And Pinky?’ She's fine too.

The Doctor says....."The fever will subside." But it hasn't.- And? said by Pappu’s wife

‘Now he wants more tests done, They are very, very expensive get them done’

Pinky asks everyday......"Where is Dad? When will he come home?"

‘I'll return when my work is over, I'll be back in 20 or 25 days’ said by Pappu

Pappu said, ‘will everything be okay? Look after Mom and Dad Look after Pinky, I will hang-up now Let's Go.’ Pappu go into his truck.

200 kilometer away on the same Highway No.8 in the car.

‘Dad, when will we reach?’ Said by David’s son

Why? Said by Poonam David’s wife ‘You didn't like Dad's dance?’

‘It's so hot in here I am bored’ Said by David’s son

‘Hey, Adi! Here's a saying, Where's your favorite spot? Pretend it's around the next corner!’ Said by David ‘don’t worry we’ll be in Athangasa soon, You'll really like it there’

My friends travel by plane. Said by Adi David’s son ‘Why don't you take me by plane?’

‘How would I do my dance in the plane?’ Said by David

Adi said ‘It's so dim here’

‘Aditya, no faces when Dad is talking!’ Said by Poona Adi’s mom

Adi! Hey Adi! David! Said ‘It's okay, chill!’

Pappu’s driver overtake David’s car and said ‘Fucker!’

‘What the fuck was he doing?’ David said

‘He didn't even look around, just kept racing ahead’

'David, they are all like that' Poonam said 'You should have slowed down'

'I was driving correctly, I can't keep slowing down' David said

'You never drive safely' Poonam said

'So you mean it was my fault? Can't we drive in peace?' David said

'Your driving makes me tense' Poonam said

'Tell me something, have I ever had an accident? Even a small one? Have I ever?' David said angrily

'Why do the two of you bicker?' Adi said

'What was that, son?'

'Nothing' Adi said

After a few minutes ago some children's are playing and singing around between kilometers of Pappu's truck

'Spin the grindstone, spin the grindstone Spin the grindstone, spin the grindstone, If the grain is ground too fine the wind blows it away And if ground too coarse no one will eat it If ground too fine the wind blows it away If ground too coarse no one will eat it' Singing by children's

A one unknown little girl are hiding behind the tree.

'Who are you? Where have you come from?' A bus driver said

'Khanbha' little girl said

'Tell me the truth' Bus driver angrily said

'Mumbai Mumbai!' little girl said

Chapter 2

‘That's very far from here’ Bus driver said to little girl

‘I want to go to Athangasa’ little girl said

‘Athangasa?’ Bus driver said

‘A truck driver was to take me and? He dropped me here and left’ little girl said

‘Look girl, do you see that highway? Go there A truck is sure to pass It'll take you’ Bus driver said

‘I'm hungry’ a little girl said

‘This is not a soup kitchen Look, you are very young, this place is not for you, Go away’ Bus driver said

‘I'm very hungry’ little girl said again and again!

On another side David stop the car on the highways Dhabha (A small place)

‘Mom, I'm thirsty’ Mom, I'm thirsty’ Adi said

‘Oh baby, what can I do? Isn't there a bottle

at your feet?’ Poonam said

Poonam sleeping well, David out of car and finds some cigarettes and Adi watch a dog around the Dhabha, He outs in car and go to the a little puppy.

‘Hail, Mother Goddess! How's business?’ David said to shopkeeper

‘It's all right’ Shopkeeper replied

90

00:13:54,669 --> 00:13:57,408

Give me a packet of

"Classic Mild" cigarettes.

‘Give me a royal stag one packet’ David said

‘I've only "Tuff 10”’ Shopkeeper replied

"Tuff 10"? What kind of joke is this?’ David replied ‘Finest tobacco!’

‘Do you have a lighter?’ David said

Now David get a cigarettes and silently get into the car and leave without watching his son.

David sons Adi follow the car and said DAD! MOM! But David cannot heard his voice. His sons follows the car around a few kilometers.

On another side of Bus driver and a little girl

‘Look, girl! As you're young.....I'll feed you for now here is your money’ But leave after that I don't want to see you after sunset Understood?’ Bus driver said to little girl

David son return back to the Dhabha and wait for David’s returning, after some hours Pappu’s truck also coming to the Dhabha! Pappu going to meet someone and his driver watching the truck. David son follows the Pappu’s driver.

‘What do you want?’ Pappu diver said

‘What you looking at? Go somewhere else and stare you loafer! Go on, scram’ Pappu driver said to Adi

Pappu wants to get some money for his sick daughter and therefore he met an Agent and sold his truck and get 25 percent of payments.

‘What took so long?’ Agent said to Pappu

‘I got delayed’ Pappu said

‘Pappu, will you ever learn! Here is proof the police have been paid’ Agent said

‘Show it if you have a problem, My cousin is back Arvind Singh Jhala He is the best His boys will be at Looniyara Give them the truck and walk away’ Agent said again

‘What will happen to my truck?’ Pappu replied

‘Don't panic Just follow instructions Here's 25 percent You'll get another 25 percent in Looniyara.....and the rest after the insurance is settled’ Agent said

‘That's fine, but what about my truck?’ Pappu replied

‘Your truck will be emptied.....and thrown off a cliff, it’s a truck, not your wife!’ Agent replied

On the another side of David and Poonam they drive car something 20 kilometers... and stop the car at Patrol pump.

Poonam said ‘wake up son’ ADI!’ Where’s Adi’

‘I'm not sure about Look between the seats’ David replied

‘Adi? He isn't in the car, David’ Poonam said

‘Hey, Adi! Adi!’ Pappu loudly called Adi at the patrol pump.

‘Have you seen a boy? He is wearing a brown shirt This tall’ David said to stranger

Stranger didn’t replied David.

David and Poonam go to nearest Police Station and complain about her missing son.

‘Name?’ Police said

-‘Poonam Shroff’ Poonam replied

‘K-I-R-A-N S-H-R-O-F-F’ ok Age’ Police said

‘- 30’ Poonam replied

‘Your child is 30?’ Police replied

‘Not my child, I'm 30’ Poonam replied

‘Who is missing? You or your child?’ Police said

‘Our son is missing’ David replied

‘I ask about the missing person and you talk about yourself! Now I have to rewrite everything When did you last see your son?’ Police said

‘Sir, we were together in the car, at Milan petrol pump’ David said

‘Did he tell you where he was going?’ Police replied

‘No, how could he?’ Poonam replied ‘He was asleep!’

‘So how did he get down?’ Police said ‘You carried him out, right?’

‘Sir, my son is old enough He can get down on his own’ Poonam replied

‘You just said the boy was asleep’ Police said

‘If you permit, I'll explain everything again’ David said

On the another side of Pappu’s Truck

‘Who is that boy?’ Agent said to Pappu

‘I don't know’ Pappu replied

‘Hey, boy! Where have you come from?’ Agent ask to Adi

‘My parents will be back’ Adi replied

‘Pappu.....take him away’ Agent said

‘Me?’ Adi said

‘Yes, Drop him to the Virdi Diner’ Agent said

‘Why do I have to deal with this kid?’ Pappu said to Agent

‘But you've got a deal with me! And I don't want him here’ Agent replied

‘Sir, I've never had kids on my truck’ Pappu said

‘There is always a first time! The Virdi Diner is open

day and night I'm sure he is that idiot's kid’ Agent replied

‘He will be there’

‘I've spoken to that man He will drop you at Virdi Diner’ Agent said to Adi

‘Please call my parents’ Adi replied

Chapter 3

‘920...920... 322......3624’ Adi give contact number of his parent to Agent

Agent dialed the number ‘But it isn't connecting I'll keep tying I've got the number now Your parents will be at Virdi Diner’ Agent said to Adi

The Truck is moving away to Virdi Dinner House

‘Hey, the truck is moving, sit down’ Truck driver said to Adi ‘Kid, what do you want?’

‘May I have some water?’ Adi replied

‘Our food is kept here Get out of the way’ Pappu’s driver said to Adi ‘Fucker!’

‘Pappu.....this kid isn't one of us We should not keep him

on our truck’ Pappu’s Driver said to Pappu

‘A dog! Pappu, now we have dogs in our truck?’ Pappu’s driver said and hurt the dog

‘Stop! You are hurting him’ Adi replied

Pappu’s driver angrily said to Adi ‘No dogs on the truck. This isn't your father's house’

‘The dog goes where I go’ Adi said

‘Good, both of you go!’ Pappu’s driver said

‘That fucker didn't say anything about the dog’ Pappu’s driver said

On the another side of Bus Driver and a little girl.

The girl met an friend who names a Rinkle in the Bus.

‘What's your name?’ Rinkle said

‘Kiran’ A little girl replied

‘I'm Rinkle Take some’ She gives some food to Kiran and replies her

‘You will like it here’ Rinkle said

‘I'll be gone by evening’ Kiran replied

‘That's what we all say in the beginning. Come, I'll show you around’ Rinkle said ‘What pretty earrings!’

‘What do you people do here?’ Kiran replied

‘We go on stage, Have you been on stage?’ Rinkle said

‘On stage? Why are you sitting there?’ Kiran replied

‘Come inside I'll tell you what we do’ Rinkle said

‘- No’ Kiran replied

‘Why? Are you scared? Don't be scared. Rajender sir won't be angy if we play here’ Rinkle replied ‘Don't be afraid You are new No one shouts at new girls’

On the another side David and The Police

‘Sir, my wife was wondering if...Sir, please can we go to

the diners? I'm sure my son is there He must be waiting for us’ David said to Police

‘Maybe...’ Police replied ‘Look, I'll send Constable Hamirbhai’

‘But it's quite far We'll go with him’ Poonam said

‘We can go in my car’ David said

‘Ok’ Police replied

On the another side of Pappu’s Truck

Pappu stop the truck at tea stoll, go to drink some tea.

‘We're having some tea You?’ Pappu’s driver said

‘No’ Adi replied

‘Okay Do what you want, It makes no difference to me’ Pappu driver said to Adi

‘Two teas, Hey! Two teas’ Pappu’s driver said to tea stoller.

‘One Cold Drink’ Pappu order and gave it to Adi.

‘What's the news? The police are everywhere’ Stranger Said

‘Where exactly?’ Pappu’s driver said

‘All over’ Stranger replied

‘- Why?’ Pappu’s driver said

‘God alone knows’ Stranger said

On the another side of Rinkle and a little girl

‘I don't want to be on stage’ said Kiran

‘Don't be silly Everyone will be on stage’ Rinkle replied ‘You love to dance, don't you?’

‘I enjoy dancing It makes me forget everything’ Kiran said

‘Then stay here’ Rinkle replies

‘- No’ Kiran replies ‘I want to go to my Grandmother's’

‘And where are your parents?’ Rinkle replies.

Chapter 4

On the another side of Poonam and Stranger

‘Sister, some hot tea For you, Don't wory, sister If the police say they will.....then they will find him,While they search Virdhi...’ Stranger gave tea to Poonam and said that

‘...why don't you take the shortcut to Chand?’ Another stranger said to Poonam

‘But the Rann, he salt desert, isn't safe’ The stranger replies to another stranger

‘It's a straight road’ Another stranger replies

‘Where does this shortcut lead to?’ Poonam said

‘Straight back onto the highway’ Stranger replies

‘On that way No But if you are careful, it's safe’ Another Stranger replies

‘She isn't familiar with the Rann.....yet you want her to drive through it?’ Stranger replies to another stranger

‘If the car is good there'll be no problem’ Stranger replies

On the another side of Pappu’s and Adi finally reached to Viridi Dinner House

‘Can you see your Dad?’ Pappu ask to Adi

‘No Dad is handsome And Mom is beautiful I don't think any of these men are fathers’ Adi replies ‘Do you have a kids’

‘I have a daughter’ Pappu’s replies

‘Doesn't she miss you?’ Adi said

‘Yes. Very much, And I miss her’ Pappu replies

‘So why aren't you with her?’ Adi ask

‘I have to work, All at home depend on me. My mother, father, wife...My daughter... Pinky’ Pappu replies

‘Pappu, why is he still here? Leave him alone We can wait a bit’ Pappu driver said

‘His parents are coming’ Pappu replies

‘Boss, we must leave, Boss, there is a police van there, I heard the police radio...Exactly like him "Missing kid"?’ Pappu’s driver said “Brown shirt, short pants, His parents have told the police, There will be police check points everywhere, We should leave this kid here’

‘Stay here both of you, I'll take a minute’ Pappu said Adi and Pappu’s driver and go to the telephone booth and call the Agent

‘Hello, it's me sir, Pappu’ Pappu said

‘Yes?’ Agent replies

‘Sir, I've reached Virdi, But the kid's parents aren't here’ Pappu said to Agent

‘Forget them, Drop the kid there, You've more important things to do’ Agent replies

‘You haven't called the parents yet?’ Pappu said

‘I've not been able to get through, Can't get through!’ Agent said

‘So what do I do now?’ Pappu replies

‘Leave the kid behind’ Agent replies ‘Cary on to Looniyara’

‘How can I? He is only 7, He is my responsibility’ Pappu replies

‘He is not your responsibility’ Agent said

‘He is on my truck, I am responsible for him’ Pappu said

‘Why are you bothered about this kid?’ Agent replies

‘My daughter is the same age’ Pappu said

‘So? He isn't your daughter’ Agent replies ‘His parents don't care, It isn't your problem, Leave now, And listen. You've taken money from me, Don't break our deal’ Agent said

‘Why bring our deal into this? I'm leaving, but the kid, has to be with his parents’ Calls ended

Then after Pappu’s Truck going to Asthagna on the Highway they stop the truck at the Police check point

‘What do we do now?’ Pappu’s driver said

“24 hours a day, 7 days a week, Day in and day out, All I do is drive, No holidays, Drive, Eat, Sleep, Drive, again and again This is all I do” Pappu says “This is my life, Nothing else”

‘Boss, what about the kid? We aren't kidnappers, but who'll believe us?’ Pappu’s driver said “The police need a scapegoat”

“What is a scapegoat?” Adi says

“Get back, you little bugger” Pappu’s driver said “Boss!”

“No matter, how well we look after him.....he'll betray us” Pappu says

“I beg you, let's dump him and cary on” Pappu’s driver said

Pappu get out of Truck

‘Remove the air filter’ Pappu said to Driver

‘For fuck's sake!, This is madness, How will we get past the police check points?, That cunt put

us in this jam’ Pappu’s driver said to Pappu

‘What is cunt?’ Adi replies

“Don't say that, It's not a nice word” Pappu said to Adi

“Where is my Dad?” Adi replies

“Boss, I say it again, let's dump him here” Pappu’s driver said

‘I will not leave a 7 year old, on this highway’ Pappu replies

“What are we to do with him?, Why did you leave your parents? Why have you come with us? Why didn't you drop me to that diner...” Pappu’s driver says to Adi

“...as that first "Uncle" said?” Adi replies

“- Fuck that "Uncle", He's no uncle, He's a pimp Agent, Fucking rich kids from the city.....going on about your "Dad", "Mom"” Pappu’s driver replies “You fucker, most of us don't have parents, We've reached the top of the hill, There is no need to be so kind to this kid, The Highway is no place to be kind, I cannot do what you want” Pappu’s driver says to Pappu

“I cannot leave him alone on, this highway” Pappu replies

‘Why?’ Pappu’s driver said “You want to adopt this kid?, That's not how you make a family, Don't your parents shout at you at times?’ Pappu’s driver replies

“No, Dad jokes, Mom laughs” Adi says to Pappu and driver

“You don't like his jokes?” Pappu replies

“No, I know all his jokes” Adi said

“Don't you like school?” Pappu ask to Adi

“No” Adi replies

“You must like something!” Pappu said

“Yes, I'm learning Karate” Adi replies

“What's Karate?” Pappu want to know about karate

“To save myself” Adi replies

“To save yourself?” Pappu said

“To save myself, From bad people” Adi replies

“Isn't there something else you learn?” Pappu want to know about Adi’s hobbies

“Well, I am in my class, "Action Song"” Adi replies

"Action Song?" Pappu said

“Yes, we sing and perform actions” Adi said

“Go on, sing it then?” Pappu want to listen song

Then Adi sing a song for Pappu

“Forget about yesterday, Yesterday's news is old, A new generation will rise, and together write a new future, We are Indians, we are Indians, We are Indians, we are Indians, Today, we have broken old shackles, Why look to destinations we have left behind?, Today we reach the moon With a new awakening, new bonds.....new blood, new hope, now we have renewed our youth We are Indians, we are Indians”

On the another side of Rinkle and a Little girl

“Don't you miss your parents?” Kiran ask to Rinkle

“Not anymore, This is my home, Our fight is on your mind? But, we love each other, I trust these girls completely” Rinkle replies

“Will someone drop me to Athangasa?” Kiran said

“Yes, someone will” Rinkle replies

After that Rinkle go on the stage

“Rinkle, please! I don't like it here, Let's go somewhere else, Please Rinkle, let's go” Kiran said to Rinkle on the stage at the time of performance

“Relax, I'll be back soon” Rinkle replies

On the another side of Pappu’s Truck

“Kid, sing that song, I like it” Pappu said to Driver and Adi and sing the song

“Forget about yesterday, Yesterday's news is old A new generation will rise, and together write a new future We are Indians, we are Indians We are Indians, We are Indians”

“Boss..I didn't know you sing so well” Pappu’s driver said to Pappu

“It reminds me of my childhood, Do you know the strange thing about my childhood? All I ever wanted was to make toys” Pappu says his childhood story to Driver and Adi

“Toys?” Adi replies

“Yes, my uncle made toys......to sell at the village fair, He used to make them at home” Pappu said

“Then?” Driver says

“Then my uncle died, I had to look for work, I was meant to make toy trucks.....now I drive a real truck, That's destiny” Pappu replies

Then after Pappu stop the truck on the road at the Police check point

“Get out on Truck” Police says to Pappu and Driver “What's inside? Anyone with you?”

“Me and my Driver” Pappu replies to Police

“What are you carying?” Police want to know what is carrying Pappu on the Truck

“Marble tiles” Pappu replies

“How much?” Police said

“6 tons” Pappu’s driver said

“You are overloaded” Police said

“No, sir! We weigh 6 tones” Pappu’s driver said

“Trying to fool me?, I can see.....your weight is not less than 10 tons, Take the Mother fuckers, to the weighing bridge We'll get the whole stock” Police replies

“Sir, please, let us go, We have paid, At Chand Diner, This truck is covered by them” Pappu’s driver says

“Who? That fucker Jadeja?” Police replies

“Yes, sir!” Pappu’s driver replies

“Give me your paas, This is last month's pass, You, sister fucker!, First you don't bribe.....and then expect to be let off? Something very funny is going on, I can smell it in your face” Police said to Pappu

“Sir! Please take this” Pappu try to gave some money to Police

“Move to the side, I don't want your loose change, I want to see.....what is going on, Let's see what the fuck is inside, Come on, get going, You are holding up everyone, Before the boss comes, get going, Come on, Keep the line moving” Police said to Pappu

“Where is he?” Pappu’s driver finds Adi on Truck

At the time of checking Adi hides on the Truck backseats

“Here, down here, Bring me up” Adi says to Driver

“You saved us, kid, You've learnt, how to hide, when to keep quiet, You have become just like us, You are one of us” Drivers says to Adi

On the another side of David and Poonam was reached to the Viridi Dinner House

“For God's sake!, I cannot find” David says to Poonam

“Where is Aditya!, Where is he? Where is my son?” Poonam ask again and again to David

“Poonam!” David satisfied to Poonam and hugging “Are you alright?”

“Where could Aditya be?”

Final Chapter

On the another side of Pappu's Truck they make some dinner on the highways side

"This is how we lead our lives, You might find our food spicy" Pappu says to Adi

"Give him some, curd and sugar" Pappu says to Driver

"Good?" Driver ask to Pappu

"Superb!, Better than home food" Adi says to Driver

"Here, have some more" Driver gave his own food too to Adi

"Do you have kids?" Adi ask to Driver

"Yes, Many" Driver replies

"Anybody like me?" Adi said

“No, Not like you, Twins, Two sets, means Girls, Didn't understand?” "With girls in the house, prosperity follows" Driver replies to Adi

On the another side of Rinkle and A little girl on the stage

Rinkle, Rinkle, Rinkle, I want to go to go, I want to go” Kiran says to Rinkle

“Kiran, Rajender sir is calling you” Some girl said to Kiran

“Where?” Kiran replies

“Come with me, Come, it's nothing, Come, I'll tell you, It's no big deal” Some girls let the kiran to Rajendra who is Bus driver

“No, No?, No I'm not going there” Kiran says to Rinkle

“Then what are you doing here?, Why aren't you going to him?, It will be over in a few minutes” Rinkle replies

“I want to go to Athangasa” Kiran says to Rinkle “My grandmother will look after me”

“What is happening?, Why are you here?” Rajendra said to Kiran

“I said "No", didn't I?” Kiran replies

“Look child......I told you not to come here, This place is not for you, You will get us into trouble, Rinkle! Why did you bring her here?” Rajendra said to Kiran and Rinkle

“I thought there'd be no harm in her being on stage” Rinkle replies

“You brought her here, now she's been picked!, Look girl, it is really, quite simple, These men are here to fuck, and you are here to be fucked, Now please, get back to work” Rajendra says what his real work on the stage and Kiran ran away on the stage, She ran away in to the Bus.

“Hey, where are you going?” Rajendra said “Listen child Stop”

On the another side of David and Poonam they reached to the Dhabha where they lost Adi and they met the owner of Dhabha who is the Agent

“We are looking for a boy, 7 years old. This tall, Has any boy like that been here?” David ask to Agent

“No, I haven't seen anyone like that” Agent replies

“Well, if you see him, remember to inform us, Call the station” Police says to Agent

“That's it? That's all you will do?” Poonam said to Police

“Madam, what do you want me to do?” Police replies

“Look! Search!, Aditya has got to be here” Poonam replies

“No, madam!, There was no kid here, You can look around if you like” Agent said to Poonam

David catch the Point

“Try and remember......from earlier today, "Hail, Goddess Mother" David said to Agent

“Are you sure this is where you stopped?” Agent said

“Yes, Remember, "I've only Tuff 10", He's lying” David said to Agent and Police

“Why are you lying? You are lying to me?, Mother Fucker! Your face tells it all” Police said to Agent

“He must be between Looniyara and Athangasa” Agen replies

On the another side of Rinkle and A little girl

“What do I do with you?, What do you want?” Rajendra said to Kiran

“Sir, I want to go to Athangasa” Kiran replies

“Child, are you sure of this?” Rajendra replies

“Yes” Kiran says

“You stay here I’ll come back” Rajendra said to Kiran and Rinkle

“Rinkle, come with me, My Grandmother will look after us, we’ll go to school together” Kiran want to Rinkle going with her

“I want to, I want to come with you” Rinkle replies

“Then come on” Kiran replies

“But this is my home, Why do you want to go back to the highway?, Where will you sleep?, Who will feed you?, Why don't you stay here?, You won't lack anything here” Rinkle says to Kiran

Then after Rajendra arrived

“Kiran, I've found someone, He will take you to Athangasa” Rajendra says to Kiran

Then Kiran goes to Athangasa with the Rajendra’s Truck driver, after that on the highway Rajendra’s

Truck driver overtaking the Pappu's truck and Pappu's truck going down on the hill.

"Pappu, save us!'" Pappu's driver says to Pappu

"What will happen to them?" Kiran says to Rajendra's Truck driver

"I don't know" Rajendra's Truck driver replies

"Please stop" Kiran says to Rajendra's Truck driver

"If we stop, we will be blamed" Rajendra's truck driver replies

"What will happen to them?" Kiran says

"Some other truck will help" Rajendra's truck driver replies

Pappu and his driver are injurious very hard but Adi is all right

"Athangasa is ahead, Do you see that crowd above? No one will move, Only the police will come down, Go with them, They'll take you to your parents, Kid! Don't tell anyone about us, We'll be in trouble, We will leave now" Pappu says to Adi and leave him

The Police wan and Adi's reached to the accident spot

“Release the kid to his parents, Make sure they are comfortable” Police says

“Come, sir!” Finally David and Poonam met Adi

“Have you noticed?, Our boy looks so grown up” Poonam says to David

On the another side of Pappu and Driver

“What will become of us, boss?” Pappu’s driver says to Pappu

“We should leave from here, It's a big county with many trucks and many highways” Pappu says to his driver

“Boss...” Pappu’s driver replies

“...I will never be able to forget this child” Last word Pappu says to his driver

And Pappu died...

www.ingramcontent.com/pod-product-compliance
Ingram Content Group UK Ltd.
Pitfield, Milton Keynes, MK11 3LW, UK
UKHW041902190726
13854UKWH00003B/1047

9 780359 218981